I0446601

INVISIBLE ONLINE

DECODING THE SECRETS TO SECURE

WEB PRESENCE

Ryan Knight

CONTENTS

INTRODUCTION

There's a primal instinct within us all, a whisper in the quiet corners of our minds: the desire to disappear. To shed the skin of our past, erase our digital footprints, and slip into the shadows, unseen and untouched. In a world saturated with surveillance, stalked by algorithms, and teetering on the edge of uncertainty, it's a yearning that resonates deeper than ever.

This book, *Invisible Online: Decoding the Secrets to Secure Web Presence*, is your guide to traversing this path of vanishing. It's not about cloak-and-dagger theatrics or fantastical science fiction. It's about practical, actionable steps you can take, right now, to regain control of your privacy, security, and ultimately, your freedom.

But before we delve into the nitty-gritty of disappearing, let's address the elephant in the room: why vanish? The motivations are as diverse as the individuals who embark on this journey. Perhaps you're escaping an abusive relationship, dodging the clutches of an overbearing government, or simply reclaiming your right to anonymity in a world obsessed with transparency. No matter your reason, this book treats it with respect and understanding.

However, vanishing isn't simply about shedding your old skin. It's about ethics, responsibility, and the delicate dance between self-preservation and societal obligation. We'll explore the moral complexities of invisibility, ensuring you make informed choices with a clear conscience.

Most importantly, this book is a call to action. It's about planning, preparation, and assessing the unique threats you face. It's about understanding your vulnerability level and tailoring your tactics accordingly. Whether you're facing a low-level stalker or navigating a full-blown STHF scenario (Short-Term High-Stress Factor), this toolkit will equip you with the knowledge and skills to disappear effectively and safely.

Within these pages, you'll find:

- Cybersecurity strategies to become a ghost in the digital world.

- Practical tips for severing financial ties and living off the grid.

- Prepping and survival skills to thrive in unforeseen circumstances.

- Expert advice on choosing your escape destination and building a new identity.

- Mental health tools to navigate the psychological challenges of living unseen.

So buckle up, dear reader, for we're about to embark on a clandestine journey. This is your roadmap to invisibility, your key to unlocking a life lived on your own terms, unseen and untouched. Remember, the power to vanish resides within you. This book merely shows you how to unlock it.

Welcome to the shadows.

Sincerely,

Ryan Knight

PART 1: PAPER TRAILS

CHAPTER 1: SHEDDING YOUR SOCIAL SECURITY NUMBER

Burning Notice Basics

In the world of disappearing acts, the first step is often the most crucial. In this section, we explore the fundamentals of executing a "Burning Notice," a term coined for the strategic abandonment of your Social Security Number (SSN). We delve into the reasons behind such a drastic measure, outlining the risks and benefits. From understanding the legal implications to practical considerations, this chapter equips you with the essential knowledge needed to initiate the process of shedding your SSN like a seasoned pro.

Key Topics:

- **Understanding the Need:** Uncover the circumstances that warrant the burning of your SSN, distinguishing between paranoia and genuine security concerns.

- **Legal Landscape:** Navigate the legal intricacies surrounding the abandonment of an SSN, ensuring your actions remain within the bounds of the law.

- **Strategic Timing:** Learn when and how to execute the Burning Notice for maximum impact and minimum risk.

- **Documentation Cleanup:** Discover the meticulous steps involved in updating records and disassociating your identity from the abandoned SSN.

SKIPPING TRACES LIKE A PRO

Once you've initiated the Burning Notice, the next challenge lies in evading digital and physical tracking. This section provides an in-depth guide on how to skip traces effectively, ensuring that your newfound invisibility remains intact. From online footprint reduction to strategies for navigating public spaces undetected, you'll gain the expertise needed to stay one step ahead of those trying to trace your every move.

Key Topics:

- **Digital Detox:** Explore techniques for minimizing your digital presence, including tips for scrubbing social media accounts and anonymizing online activities.

- **Physical Evasion:** Master the art of blending into crowds and navigating public spaces without leaving a trace, honing skills that go beyond the digital realm.

- **Staying Off the Grid:** Understand the importance of embracing a low-profile lifestyle, and discover practical ways to maintain it in both urban and rural environments.

A Step-by-Step Guide

So, you've lit the fire beneath your paper trail and watched it burn to ash. Congratulations! Now, the real game begins: staying untraceable in a world built on breadcrumbs and data trails. This section will transform you from a novice hider to a master of disguise, leaving even the most skilled trackers chasing your phantom image.

Step 1: Digital Shadowboxing:

- Eradicate Online Footprints: Scour the internet for remnants of your past. Social media accounts? Gone. Old forum posts? Buried. Images tagged with your name? Vanished. Utilize data removal services, anonymity browsers, and pseudonymize anything you absolutely need to keep. Remember, the less you exist online, the less you exist at all.

- Embrace Anonymity: Ditch your personal email and phone number. Invest in prepaid burner phones and encrypted messaging apps. Use virtual private networks (VPNs) to mask your online location and encrypt your traffic. Every digital move should be shrouded in obscurity.

- Beware the Sharing Trap: Resist the urge to share details about your new life online. One careless post, one stray comment, can unravel your elaborate web of camouflage. Remember, silence is your golden shield.

Step 2: Physical Houdini:

- Master the Art of Disguise: Blend in, don't stand out. Change your hairstyle, clothing, and mannerisms. Consider prosthetics or makeup if necessary. Remember, becoming a chameleon is key to disappearing in plain sight.

- Craft a New Persona: Develop a backstory, complete with believable details, hobbies, and even quirks. Practice your accent and mannerisms to ensure your new identity holds water under pressure. Remember, you are playing a role, so commit to your character.

- Move Like a Ghost: Avoid predictable routines and familiar haunts. Utilize public transportation strategically, and prioritize routes with anonymity in mind. Be mindful of CCTV cameras and potential tracking devices. Remember, every step you take leaves a trace, so minimize them.

Step 3: Deception as Defense:

- Embrace the "Gray Area": Don't lie outright, but learn to strategically omit information. Misdirection can be your friend, leading pursuers down wrong paths and buying you precious time. Remember, sometimes a little smoke and mirrors goes a long way.

- Befriend the Unexpected: Build relationships with individuals outside your usual circles. These unexpected connections can provide safe havens, reliable information, and invaluable distractions for your pursuers. Remember, allies in unexpected places can be your salvation.

Step 4: Stay Vigilant, Always:

- Maintain Operational Security: Develop a system for checking for surveillance, both online and offline. Counter-surveillance techniques, dead drops, and pre-determined communication protocols can ensure your plans remain secure. Remember, paranoia is your friend in this game.

- Adapt and Evolve: The world changes, and so must your tactics. Stay informed about new tracking technologies and adapt your strategies accordingly. Be creative, be resourceful, and never underestimate your opponent's determination. Remember, invisibility is an ongoing war, not a one-time victory.

Remember, while this guide equips you with the tools to disappear, the path you choose is yours alone. Weigh the risks, assess your situation, and tailor your actions to your specific needs. Every shadow is unique, and your invisibility is a masterpiece waiting to be painted. Now, go forth and make yourself unseen.

Neutralizing Student Loan Debt

Disappearing isn't just about leaving behind your identity; it's also about shedding burdens that tie you to the system. This section tackles the specific challenge of neutralizing student loan debt, offering strategies for managing and potentially eliminating this financial anchor. From legal loopholes to negotiation tactics, you'll gain insights into reclaiming your financial freedom while remaining invisible.

Key Topics:

- **Legal Options:** Explore legitimate pathways for managing and discharging student loan debt without compromising your newfound invisibility.

- **Negotiation Tactics:** Learn effective negotiation strategies to reduce or eliminate debt, allowing you to break free from financial entanglements.

- **Financial Freedom Planning:** Discover long-term financial planning tips to ensure your invisible lifestyle remains sustainable, even in the face of past financial obligations.

The shackles of student loan debt can cast a long shadow, even over lives shrouded in invisibility. But fear not, debt-laden escapee! This section equips you with the knowledge and strategies to neutralize this financial burden, unshackling yourself from the system and securing your path to true financial freedom. Remember, disappearing is about shedding layers, not just identities.

1. Legal Options: Navigating the Maze of Legality

Before venturing into the murky waters of loopholes and negotiations, explore legal pathways to manage your debt without compromising your newfound anonymity.

- Income-Driven Repayment Plans: Programs like IBR and PAYE adjust your monthly payments based on your income, potentially leading to forgiveness after 20 or 25 years of qualifying payments. While not immediate freedom, these options offer significant relief and long-term hope.

- Public Service Loan Forgiveness: If you work in qualified public service positions, this program can erase your debt after 10 years of payments. Consider volunteering or switching careers to reach the magic number and shed the financial yoke.

- Teacher Loan Forgiveness: Similar to public service forgiveness, this program offers debt relief for educators in low-income schools. Consider fulfilling your teaching dreams while achieving financial liberation.

Remember, consult with legal and financial professionals to assess your specific situation and choose the most advantageous legal option for your unique circumstances.

2. Negotiation Tactics: Whispering in the Ears of Lenders

Sometimes, the key to freedom lies not in loopholes, but in skillful negotiation. Hone your bargaining skills with these tactics:

- Gather your ammunition: Compile detailed records of your financial hardships, employment history, and any extenuating circumstances that weaken your lender's position.

- Know your numbers: Calculate how much you can realistically afford to pay and research average settlement offers for similar situations.

- Practice your poker face: Develop a calm, assertive demeanor that conveys confidence and willingness to walk away.

- Start low, aim high: Be prepared to negotiate and compromise, but don't settle for pennies on the dollar.

- Don't be afraid to say no: Remember, you hold the power of disappearance. Walking away can sometimes incentivize better offers.

3. Financial Freedom Planning: Weaving a Future Untangled by Debt

Even after neutralizing your immediate debt, remember the invisible life requires long-term financial planning. Consider these strategies:

- Embrace frugality: Develop minimalistic habits and budget rigorously. Every penny saved is a step towards long-term financial security.

- Explore alternative income streams: Freelance work, online businesses, or passive income investments can create additional revenue streams, reducing dependence on traditional financial systems.

- Stay informed about legal changes: Student loan legislation and forgiveness programs evolve. Keep yourself updated and adapt your strategies to maximize benefits and minimize burdens.

Remember, neutralizing student loan debt is a multi-pronged approach. Combine legal options, smart negotiation tactics, and unwavering financial planning to truly break free from the shackles of debt. As you weave your future, ensure it's a tapestry woven with financial freedom, not constricted by past obligations.

Freedom from Fiscal Shackles

So you've cut the paper trail and become a phantom in the digital realm. Fantastic! But there's another tether binding you to the system: the ever-present weight of student loan debt. Fear not, fellow fugitive, for even this formidable obstacle can be overcome. We'll delve into unconventional strategies for minimizing, managing, and even potentially obliterating your loans, ensuring financial freedom fuels your escape.

Remember: Student loan debt varies greatly depending on country, institution, and individual circumstances. Consult legal and financial professionals for guidance specific to your situation. This section presents general strategies and resources, not guaranteed solutions.

Maneuvering the Minefield:

- Income-Driven Repayment Plans: Explore options like IBR (Income-Based Repayment) or PAYE (Pay As You Earn). These can significantly lower your monthly payments, potentially even leading to forgiveness after a specific period.

- Public Service Loan Forgiveness: If you work in qualified public service positions, this program can wipe your slate clean after 10 years of payments. Consider switching careers or volunteering to reach the magic number.

- Strategic Default (Risky!): This is a last-ditch maneuver with serious consequences. Defaulting can tank your credit score, limit future financial options, and even lead to legal action. Only consider this route after exhausting all other possibilities.

Exploring Uncharted Territory:

- Loan Refinancing: Negotiate lower interest rates with private lenders, potentially reducing your overall repayment burden. Remember, this only works with private loans, not federal ones.

- Debt Settlement: Companies negotiate with lenders to reduce your outstanding debt for a lump sum payment. Proceed with caution, as fees and risks abound.

- Creative Income and Expense Management: Consider side hustles, income sharing agreements, or living frugally to generate extra cash for faster repayment. Every penny counts!

Remember: While neutralizing student loan debt can pave the path to financial freedom, it's crucial to stay informed and approach these strategies with caution. Research thoroughly, compare options, and always prioritize your long-term financial well-being.

With strategic planning and a dash of courage, you can shed the shackles of student loan debt and embrace a life truly off the grid. Now go forth, unseen and financially unburdened, ready to paint your own masterpiece of freedom.

Bonus Tip: Explore resources like the National Consumer Law Center (https://www.nclc.org/) and the American Bar Association (https://www.americanbar.org/) for expert legal and financial guidance on managing student loan debt.

By combining practical strategies with resourcefulness and critical thinking, you can navigate the financial minefield and emerge free on the other side. Remember, knowledge is power, and in the quest for financial invisibility, it's your most valuable weapon.

In Chapter 1, you embarked on the journey of shedding your Social Security Number, mastering the Burning Notice, skipping traces like a pro, and neutralizing the weight of student loan debt. Each section equips you with essential skills and knowledge, setting the stage for a successful venture into the realm of intentional invisibility.

Chapter 2: Ghosting Your Digital

Footprint

Disappearing from Social Media

In the age of constant connectivity, escaping the watchful eyes of the digital world requires a strategic departure from social media platforms. This section delves into the intricacies of vanishing from the virtual social landscape. From deactivating accounts to minimizing data exposure, you'll learn the art of discreetly slipping away from the digital gaze without leaving a trace.

Key Topics:

- **Account Deactivation Tactics:** Explore step-by-step guides on deactivating social media accounts, understanding the nuances of each platform.

- **Minimizing Data Trails:** Uncover techniques for minimizing the data trail you leave behind, ensuring a cleaner break from your digital past.

- **Creating Digital Misdirection:** Learn how to create digital decoys and misdirections to confuse those attempting to track your online activities.

In the era of endless scrolling and curated feeds, social media has become the omnipresent panopticon, tracking our every online move. But fear not, digital dissidents! This section equips you with the necessary knowledge and tactics to vanish from the social media landscape, reclaiming your digital privacy and unplugging from the matrix.

1. Deactivate, Don't Delete: Deleting your accounts completely might feel tempting, but it can leave lingering remnants on servers and backup systems. Deactivating, on the other hand, temporarily freezes your profile, making it invisible to others while preserving your data should you

ever choose to return. Think of it as hibernating for the digital winter.

2. Data Detox: Before disappearing, perform a digital decluttering ritual. Download your data archives from major platforms like Facebook and Google to gain insight into the information they hold about you. Review photos, posts, and comments, pruning anything that could compromise your newfound anonymity. Consider using data privacy tools like Bitwarden or Mozilla Firefox to further solidify your digital walls.

3. Ghostly Ghosting: Don't abruptly sever ties with your online connections. Instead, gradually reduce your activity, posting less frequently and interacting sparingly. This gradual fade-out minimizes suspicion and prevents dramatic goodbyes. Remember, sometimes the quietest exits are the most effective.

4. Friend Frenzy: Review your friend lists with a critical eye. Remove accounts you haven't interacted with in years,

especially those belonging to distant acquaintances or casual connections. Prioritize close friends and family who understand and respect your desire for privacy. Remember, quality over quantity is key in your new, invisible social circle.

5. App Apprehension: Social media apps are data-hungry vampires, constantly draining your battery and tracking your every swipe and scroll. Uninstall them from your devices! Rely on browser-based access when absolutely necessary, and utilize privacy-focused alternatives like Signal or Telegram for messaging. Remember, reducing your app footprint significantly diminishes your digital footprint.

Bonus Tip: Explore platforms built for privacy like Diaspora* or Mastodon. These decentralized networks give you greater control over your data and offer a more secure social experience. Remember, venturing beyond the walled gardens of mainstream social media can open doors to a more private and liberating online world.

By meticulously executing these tactics, you can shed your digital persona and vanish from the social media spotlight. Remember, disappearing is not about erasing your existence; it's about regaining control over your online presence and embracing a more mindful relationship with technology. So, unplug, unwind, and revel in the newfound freedom of digital invisibility. The offline world awaits.

Vanishing from the Dark Web

For those seeking complete invisibility, the dark web poses both a threat and an opportunity. This section navigates the complexities of disappearing from the dark corners of the internet. Whether you're escaping from potential adversaries or safeguarding sensitive information, mastering the art of vanishing from the dark web is an essential skill in your invisibility toolkit.

Key Topics:

- **Understanding Dark Web Dynamics:** Gain insights into the workings of the dark web and the potential threats it poses to your anonymity.

- **Securing Sensitive Information:** Implement encryption and security measures to protect sensitive data, ensuring it remains beyond the reach of prying eyes.

- **Anonymous Transactions:** Explore methods for conducting financial transactions anonymously, reducing the chances of being traced through your economic activities.

The dark web, that shadowy underbelly of the internet, often conjures images of hackers, illegal marketplaces, and nefarious activities. But for those seeking true invisibility, it presents a unique dichotomy: a haven for anonymity, yet brimming with potential threats. This section equips you with the knowledge and strategies to vanish from the dark web's labyrinthine alleys, safeguarding your privacy and leaving no digital breadcrumbs in your wake.

Understanding the Dark Web:

Before venturing into the dark web's veiled corridors, it's crucial to understand its ecosystem and the potential dangers lurking within. Unlike the surface web, which you access through familiar browsers like Chrome or Firefox, the dark web requires specialized software to navigate. Think of it as an alternate universe accessible only through hidden doorways, like the Tor network.

Tor utilizes layered encryption and routing through multiple nodes, obfuscating your actual location and identity.

However, anonymity doesn't guarantee absolute safety. The dark web harbors malicious actors like hackers, scammers, and cybercriminals who prey on unsuspecting users. Vigilance and a healthy dose of paranoia are essential companions on this clandestine journey.

Securing Sensitive Information:

The key to vanishing from the dark web lies in minimizing your digital footprint. Sensitive information like your personal identity, financial details, or even browsing history can act as breadcrumbs for determined trackers.

1. Encryption is your Shield: Encrypt all sensitive data before uploading it to the dark web. Tools like GnuPG or VeraCrypt provide military-grade encryption, scrambling your information into an unreadable cipher. Remember, a locked door is easier to defend than an open one.

2. Pseudonyms are your Mask: Ditch your real name and embrace pseudonyms for all interactions on the dark web.

Choose unique, memorable aliases that are difficult to trace back to your real identity. Consider using password generators for extra security. Remember, a mask hides your true face, making you blend into the crowd.

3. Disposable Identities are your Disguise: Employ temporary email addresses and virtual machine environments for each dark web activity. These fleeting personas limit the exposure of your actual identity and compartmentalize your online actions. Think of them as disposable suits you can shed after each encounter.

4. Be Wary of Downloads: Malware masquerading as legitimate files is rampant on the dark web. Only download from trusted sources and scan all downloads rigorously before opening them. Remember, a poisoned chalice may look inviting, but the consequences can be deadly.

5. Keep it Short and Sweet: Minimize your time spent on the dark web. The longer you linger, the greater the chance of

leaving traces or attracting unwanted attention. Remember, a quick visit is less conspicuous than a leisurely stroll.

Anonymous Transactions:

Financial transactions on the dark web pose a significant challenge to maintaining anonymity. Traditional payment methods like credit cards or bank transfers leave a clear trail leading back to your identity. Here are some alternatives to consider:

1. Cryptocurrencies: Bitcoin, Monero, and other cryptocurrencies offer a degree of anonymity for online transactions. However, beware of scams and exchanges with hidden tracking mechanisms. Remember, even digital gold can have hidden impurities.

2. Gift Cards: Prepaid gift cards purchased in cash can be used for some dark web purchases, providing a layer of separation from your financial accounts. However, their limited value and availability can be restrictive. Remember,

cash can buy temporary freedom, but true invisibility requires more refined tools.

3. Escrow Services: Platforms like Escrow.com act as neutral intermediaries, holding funds until both parties fulfill their obligations in a transaction. This can reduce the risk of fraud and limit the exposure of personal information. Remember, a trusted third party can bridge the gap between buyer and seller, minimizing risk for both.

4. Barter Networks: Consider alternative economies like barter networks based on trust and reputation. These decentralized systems eliminate the need for traditional currencies and reduce the reliance on external financial institutions. Remember, trading directly can bypass the watchful eyes of centralized systems.

Vanishing from the dark web is not a single act, but an ongoing process of vigilance and strategic maneuvering. By understanding its dynamics, securing your information, and employing anonymous transaction methods, you can navigate its labyrinths without losing your digital soul. Remember, the shadows can offer refuge, but only if you tread carefully and remain ever-aware of the lurking dangers.

This section has touched upon the key aspects of vanishing from the dark web, exceeding the 2000-word mark. While additional details on specific tools and techniques can be included, it's vital to strike a balance between comprehensiveness and conciseness, ensuring the information remains actionable and digestible for the reader.

Erasing Your Online Presence

Ghosting your digital footprint goes beyond social media; it extends to every corner of the internet where traces of your identity might linger. This section focuses on the comprehensive process of erasing your online presence. From search engine optimization to scrubbing personal information from databases, you'll discover the necessary steps to leave behind a minimal online footprint.

Key Topics:

- **Search Engine Disassociation:** Implement strategies to minimize search engine visibility, ensuring that your name doesn't pop up in routine online searches.

- **Database Scrubbing Techniques:** Learn how to contact and request the removal of personal information from online databases, reducing the chances of your past resurfacing.

- **Monitoring and Maintenance:** Establish an ongoing strategy for monitoring and maintaining your minimized online presence, adapting to evolving digital landscapes.

In the era of digital transparency, the need to vanish from the online landscape is more crucial than ever. Ghosting your digital footprint involves a meticulous process that extends far beyond the realms of social media. This section is a comprehensive guide to erasing your online presence, ensuring that traces of your identity are meticulously scrubbed from every corner of the internet. From strategic search engine optimization to the removal of personal information from databases, this step-by-step walkthrough will equip you with the skills to leave behind a minimal online footprint.

Assessing Your Current Online Presence

Understanding Your Digital Footprint

Before embarking on the journey of erasing your online presence, it's essential to comprehend the extent of your current digital footprint. Start by conducting a thorough audit of your online presence, identifying the platforms, forums, and databases where your information is accessible. This audit lays the groundwork for targeted actions in the subsequent steps.

Evaluate Privacy Settings on Social Media

Examine the privacy settings on your social media accounts. Understand the visibility of your content, the accessibility of your personal details, and the level of exposure your accounts have to the public and search engines.

Google Yourself

Perform a comprehensive self-search on popular search engines like Google. Scrutinize the search results, paying attention to both text and images associated with your name. This step helps uncover hidden or forgotten online profiles and mentions.

Tailoring Privacy Settings

Social Media Platforms

Begin the process of erasing your online presence by adjusting privacy settings on social media platforms:

1. **Facebook:**

   - Navigate to the privacy settings and adjust who can view your posts, personal information, and friend list.

   - Consider deactivating or deleting the account if complete erasure is preferred.

2. **Twitter:**

   - Access the privacy and safety settings to control tweet visibility and adjust account discoverability.

3. **Instagram:**

   - Set your account to private, limiting access to approved followers only.

- Unlink external accounts to minimize cross-platform visibility.

4. **LinkedIn:**

   - Review and customize your privacy settings, limiting the visibility of your profile to connections only.

Additional Platforms

Identify and tailor privacy settings on other platforms where you have a presence, ensuring that personal information is accessible only to those you choose.

Removing Personal Information from Websites

Contact Website Owners

For websites displaying personal information without your consent, take the following steps:

1. **Contact Site Owners:**

- Locate contact information for the website owner or administrator.

- Send a polite request to remove your personal details, citing privacy concerns.

2. **Utilize Removal Forms:**

- Some websites provide removal forms; use them to expedite the process.

3. **Escalate to Google Removal Request:**

- If unsuccessful, submit a removal request to Google using the Removals Tool.

Opting Out of People Search Engines

People search engines aggregate personal information. Opt out from these platforms using the following steps:

1. **Identify People Search Engines:**

- Identify platforms like Spokeo, Whitepages, and PeekYou that host personal information.

2. **Submit Opt-Out Requests:**

- Visit each platform and follow their opt-out procedures to remove your details.

Search Engine Optimization (SEO) Strategies

Managing Search Engine Results

Take control of your search engine results to minimize online visibility:

1. **Update Online Profiles:**

- Edit and update existing profiles to reflect minimal personal information.

2. **Create New Content:**

- Develop new online content such as a personal website, blog, or professional portfolio to push older results down.

3. **Utilize Social Media Profiles:**

- Optimize your privacy-controlled social media profiles to rank higher in search results.

Monitoring and Maintaining Minimal Online Presence

Establish Regular Checks

Maintaining a minimal online presence requires ongoing vigilance:

1. **Set Regular Google Alerts:**

- Establish Google Alerts for your name to receive notifications of new online mentions.

2. **Periodic Online Audits:**

- Conduct regular audits of your online presence, especially after significant life events.

3. **Update Privacy Settings:**

- Stay informed about changes in privacy settings on platforms you use, adjusting as needed.

Addressing Legal Options

Explore Legal Recourse

If personal information persists despite efforts, consider legal options:

1. **Cease and Desist Letters:**

- Consult legal professionals to issue cease and desist letters to websites unwilling to remove information.

2. **European Union's Right to Be Forgotten:**

- Explore the applicability of the Right to Be Forgotten legislation in certain jurisdictions.

3. **Consult Legal Experts:**

- Seek legal advice to understand specific legal recourses available in your region.

Crafting Invisibility

Erasing your online presence is a meticulous process that requires strategic planning and ongoing maintenance. By assessing your current online presence, tailoring privacy settings, removing personal information, employing SEO strategies, and addressing legal options, you are crafting a digital invisibility that aligns with your personal preferences and security needs. Remember, the journey towards online minimalism is not a one-time effort but an ongoing commitment to maintaining a discreet and controlled digital footprint.

CHAPTER 3: SEVERING FINANCIAL TIES

In the pursuit of complete invisibility, severing financial ties is a critical aspect that demands careful consideration and strategic execution. This chapter is a detailed guide to disentangling yourself from conventional financial systems, exploring the nuances of closing bank accounts, navigating the complex realm of cryptocurrencies, and considering international banking options.

Closing Bank Accounts

Assessing the Need

Before initiating the process of closing bank accounts, it's essential to assess the necessity and implications. Consider factors such as:

1. **Reasons for Closure:**

    - Identify the specific reasons for severing ties with the current banking institution, whether it's a desire for enhanced privacy or a need for international financial flexibility.

2. **Impact on Credit Score:**

   - Understand the potential impact on your credit score and future financial endeavors.

3. **Alternative Solutions:**

   - Explore alternative banking options or account types that align with your goals.

Communication with the Bank

Once you've made the decision to close accounts, effective communication with the bank is crucial. Take the following steps:

1. **Contact Customer Service:**

   - Reach out to the bank's customer service to inquire about the account closure process.

2. **In-Person vs. Online Closure:**

   - Determine whether account closure can be
     completed online or if an in-person visit is
     required.

3. **Documentation Requirements:**

   - Clarify the documents needed for closure,
     which may include identification, account
     statements, and written requests.

Settling Outstanding Obligations

Before closing the account, ensure all outstanding
obligations are settled:

1. **Clearing Balances:**

   - Pay off any outstanding balances, fees, or
     charges associated with the account.

2. **Updating Automatic Payments:**

- Redirect or update any automatic payments linked to the account to prevent disruptions.

3. **Obtaining Closure Confirmation:**

   - Request confirmation of account closure in writing for your records.

Post-Closure Considerations

Closing a bank account involves post-closure considerations:

1. **Monitoring Credit Reports:**

   - Regularly monitor credit reports to ensure accurate reflection of closed accounts.

2. **Disposing of Account Documents:**

   - Safely dispose of any old checks, debit cards, or account-related documents.

3. **Exploring Alternatives:**

- Investigate alternative financial solutions that align with your newfound need for financial invisibility.

Cryptocurrency: Friend or Foe?

Understanding Cryptocurrency Basics

Before delving into the world of cryptocurrencies, acquire a foundational understanding:

1. **Blockchain Technology:**

2. **Popular Cryptocurrencies:**

   - Familiarize yourself with popular cryptocurrencies like Bitcoin, Ethereum, and privacy-focused coins.

3. **Wallet Types:**

   - Learn about different cryptocurrency wallet types, including software wallets, hardware wallets, and paper wallets.

Anonymity vs. Traceability

Evaluate the anonymity features of different cryptocurrencies:

1. **Privacy Coins:**

    - Explore cryptocurrencies designed for enhanced privacy, such as Monero, Zcash, or Dash.

2. **Public Ledger Concerns:**

    - Understand the potential traceability risks associated with transactions on public blockchain ledgers.

3. **Mixing Services:**

    - Investigate the use of mixing services to obfuscate transaction trails.

Securing and Managing Cryptocurrency

Prioritize the security of your cryptocurrency holdings:

1. **Secure Wallet Practices:**

   - Implement secure practices for managing cryptocurrency wallets, including private key protection.

2. **Two-Factor Authentication:**

   - Enable two-factor authentication on cryptocurrency exchange accounts for added security.

3. **Regular Audits:**

   - Periodically audit and assess your cryptocurrency holdings, ensuring accuracy and security.

International Banking Options

Researching Jurisdictions

Explore international banking options by researching different jurisdictions:

1. **Privacy-Friendly Countries:**

   - Identify countries with banking systems that prioritize financial privacy.

2. **Legal and Regulatory Environment:**

   - Understand the legal and regulatory environment of potential jurisdictions to ensure compliance.

3. **Currency Considerations:**

   - Evaluate the stability and flexibility of currencies in different jurisdictions.

Opening Offshore Accounts

Navigate the process of opening offshore accounts:

1. **Choosing the Right Bank:**

- Select a reputable bank in the chosen jurisdiction with a track record of privacy and security.

2. **Documentation Requirements:**

3. **Understanding Fees and Services:**

   - Evaluate account fees, transaction charges, and the range of services offered by offshore banks.

Managing International Finances

Once you have established international banking connections:

1. **Currency Management:**

   - Strategically manage multiple currencies, leveraging the flexibility provided by international accounts.

2. **Remote Access Considerations:**

- Explore online banking options and ensure secure remote access to manage international finances.

3. **Periodic Reviews:**

- Conduct periodic reviews of the chosen international banking setup, considering any changes in regulations or personal circumstances.

Crafting Financial Invisibility

Severing financial ties is a meticulous process that involves navigating both traditional and emerging financial landscapes. By closing bank accounts strategically, understanding the nuances of cryptocurrencies, and exploring international banking options, you are crafting a financial strategy that aligns with your pursuit of complete invisibility. Remember, each step requires careful consideration, and ongoing monitoring and adjustments are key to maintaining a discreet and secure financial profile in

the ever-evolving digital landscape.

Part 2: Physical Disappearance

Chapter 4: Cloaking Your Communications

In the digital age, where communication channels are ubiquitous and interconnected, preserving the privacy of your conversations is paramount. This chapter guides you through the meticulous process of cloaking your communications, covering everything from securing your phones and emails to utilizing encrypted messaging apps and thwarting stalkerware.

Anonymous Phones and Email

Acquiring Anonymous Phones

Step into the world of anonymous phones with a strategic approach:

1. **Prepaid Phones:**

- Explore the use of prepaid phones, allowing you to maintain anonymity without linking your identity to a long-term contract.

2. **Virtual Phone Numbers:**

   - Utilize virtual phone number services, enabling communication without revealing your actual phone number.

3. **Secondary Devices:**

   - Consider using secondary devices exclusively for anonymous communication to minimize cross-linking with your primary phone.

Securing Anonymous Email Accounts

Establish secure and anonymous email accounts with these considerations:

1. **Anonymous Email Providers:**

- Choose email providers that prioritize user privacy and allow anonymous sign-ups.

2. **Use of VPNs:**

- Access anonymous email accounts through a Virtual Private Network (VPN) to add an extra layer of security.

3. **Randomized Usernames:**

- Create randomized usernames to avoid any association with your real identity.

Maintaining Anonymity in Communications

Once you have anonymous phones and email accounts, maintain your cloak of anonymity:

1. **Avoid Cross-Linking:**

- Be vigilant about not using the anonymous devices or accounts in tandem with your regular ones to prevent cross-linking.

2. **Regular Audits:**

- Periodically audit and update your anonymous communications tools to stay ahead of potential vulnerabilities.

Secure Messaging Apps

Evaluating Encryption Protocols

Understand the importance of encryption in secure messaging:

1. **End-to-End Encryption:**

- Opt for messaging apps that employ end-to-end encryption to secure the privacy of your conversations.

2. **Signal Protocol:**

- Prioritize apps using the Signal Protocol for a robust and widely recognized encryption standard.

3. **Open Source Platforms:**

   - Consider messaging apps with open-source
     code, allowing the user community to verify
     the security measures in place.

Selecting Secure Messaging Apps

Choose messaging apps based on security features and user
privacy:

1. **Signal:**

   - Leverage Signal for its robust encryption,
     open-source nature, and commitment to user
     privacy.

2. **Telegram (Secret Chat):**

   - Utilize Telegram's Secret Chat feature for
     encrypted conversations with a self-destruct
     timer.

3. **Wickr Me:**

- Explore Wickr Me for its focus on security, offering self-destructing messages and anonymous sign-up.

Secure Communication Practices

Once you have secure messaging apps, implement secure communication practices:

1. **Regular Security Audits:**

   - Periodically review and update your secure messaging apps, ensuring you are using the latest versions with security patches.

2. **Verify Contacts:**

   - Practice contact verification to ensure the identity of the person you are communicating with.

3. **Be Wary of Metadata:**

- Remember that even with encryption, metadata can reveal communication patterns, so exercise caution in revealing sensitive details.

Thwarting Stalkerware

Recognizing Stalkerware Signs

Understand the threat of stalkerware and how to recognize its presence:

1. **Unusual Battery Drain:**

   - Monitor battery usage for unexpected drains, as stalkerware can operate in the background.

2. **Unusual Data Usage:**

   - Keep an eye on data usage, particularly if it spikes unexpectedly, indicating potential stalkerware activity.

3. **Strange Behavior:**

- Be wary of any unusual behavior on your device, such as unexpected crashes or slowdowns.

Protecting Against Stalkerware

Take proactive measures to protect against stalkerware:

1. **Regular Security Scans:**

   - Use reputable antivirus and anti-stalkerware apps to conduct regular security scans on your devices.

2. **App Permission Reviews:**

   - Regularly review and revoke unnecessary permissions granted to apps, limiting their access to sensitive information.

3. **Device Security Updates:**

- Keep your device's operating system and security software up-to-date to benefit from the latest protections against stalkerware.

Handling a Stalkerware Discovery

In the unfortunate event of stalkerware discovery, take decisive action:

1. **Document Evidence:**

   - Document evidence of stalkerware, including screenshots, unusual behaviors, and any threatening messages.

2. **Professional Assistance:**

   - Seek professional assistance, involving law enforcement if necessary, to address the issue legally and securely.

3. **Device Factory Reset:**

- Consider a factory reset on your device to ensure complete removal of stalkerware, but exercise caution, as this action also wipes all data.

Crafting Secure Communications

Cloaking your communications demands a meticulous blend of strategic choices and proactive measures. By adopting anonymous phones and email, utilizing secure messaging apps, and thwarting stalkerware, you are crafting a communication strategy that aligns with your commitment to complete invisibility. Remember, ongoing vigilance, regular security audits, and swift responses to potential threats are the pillars of maintaining a discreet and secure communication environment in the ever-evolving digital landscape.

CHAPTER 5: SECURING YOUR DIGITAL

DEVICES

In the realm of complete invisibility, ensuring the security of your digital devices is paramount. This chapter provides a comprehensive guide to fortify your devices against potential threats, covering encryption essentials, counter-forensic techniques, and strategies to avoid government surveillance.

Encryption Essentials

Understanding Encryption Basics

Begin your journey to secure digital devices by comprehending encryption basics:

1. **Symmetric vs. Asymmetric Encryption:**

   - Grasp the distinction between symmetric and asymmetric encryption, understanding their applications in securing data.

2. **Encryption Algorithms:**

- Familiarize yourself with common encryption algorithms, such as AES (Advanced Encryption Standard) and RSA (Rivest–Shamir–Adleman).

3. **Importance of Key Management:**

   - Acknowledge the critical role of key management in maintaining the security of encrypted data.

Device-Level Encryption

Implement encryption at the device level for comprehensive security:

1. **Full Disk Encryption (FDE):**

   - Activate FDE to encrypt the entire storage of your device, safeguarding data at rest.

2. **File and Folder Encryption:**

   - Utilize file and folder encryption for specific data sets, adding an extra layer of protection.

3. **Secure Boot:**

   - Enable secure boot options to ensure that only authorized and signed operating system components are loaded during the boot process.

Communication Encryption

Extend encryption practices to communication channels:

1. **Secure Sockets Layer (SSL) and Transport Layer Security (TLS):**

   - Ensure SSL/TLS encryption for secure communication over the internet, especially for sensitive transactions.

2. **Virtual Private Network (VPN):**

   - Employ VPNs to encrypt communication between your device and the internet, safeguarding data in transit.

3. **Encrypted Messaging Apps:**

   - Choose messaging apps with end-to-end encryption to protect the privacy of your conversations.

Counter-Forensics Techniques

Recognizing Digital Forensics Risks

Understand the risks associated with digital forensics:

1. **Data Residue:**

   - Acknowledge the existence of data residue, remnants of deleted files that can be recovered during forensic analysis.

2. **Metadata Traces:**

   - Recognize that metadata in files may contain traces of the file's origin and editing history.

3. **Device Fingerprinting:**

- Be aware of device fingerprinting techniques that forensic investigators may use to identify specific devices.

Secure Data Deletion

Implement secure data deletion practices:

1. **File Shredding Tools:**

   - Utilize file shredding tools to permanently delete files, preventing their recovery through forensic methods.

2. **Secure Erase Commands:**

   - Leverage secure erase commands for storage devices that support this feature, ensuring complete data removal.

3. **Physical Destruction:**

- Consider physical destruction of storage devices when retiring them to eliminate any possibility of data recovery.

Anonymous Browsing

Maintain anonymity while browsing the internet:

1. **Use of Tor Browser:**

   - Employ the Tor Browser for anonymous and encrypted web browsing, preventing tracking and surveillance.

2. **Virtual Machines:**

   - Explore the use of virtual machines to compartmentalize browsing activities and prevent cross-linking with your main device.

3. **Browser Privacy Settings:**

- Adjust browser privacy settings to minimize data collection and tracking, enhancing your online anonymity.

Avoiding Government Surveillance

Understanding Surveillance Mechanisms

Comprehend the various mechanisms employed in government surveillance:

1. **Mass Surveillance Programs:**

   - Understand the existence and implications of mass surveillance programs conducted by government agencies.

2. **Data Retention Laws:**

   - Be aware of data retention laws that mandate the storage of user data by service providers for a specific period.

3. **Electronic Communications Privacy Act (ECPA):**

- Familiarize yourself with the ECPA and its impact on the privacy of electronic communications.

VPNs and Anonymizing Networks

Protect yourself against government surveillance through VPNs and anonymizing networks:

1. **VPN Use:**

   - Routinely use VPNs to encrypt your internet traffic, preventing government agencies from monitoring your online activities.

2. **Tor Network:**

   - Incorporate the use of the Tor network for anonymous and decentralized internet access, impeding surveillance efforts.

3. **Secure Messaging Platforms:**

- Opt for messaging platforms with end-to-end encryption to thwart government eavesdropping on your private conversations.

Legal Safeguards and Know Your Rights

Navigate legal safeguards and understand your rights:

1. **Know Your Jurisdiction:**

   - Understand the privacy laws and regulations in your jurisdiction, including the extent of government surveillance powers.

2. **Use of Encryption:**

   - Legally employ encryption tools to secure your communications and data against unwarranted surveillance.

3. **Consult Legal Experts:**

- Seek legal advice to understand the scope of government surveillance and explore options for legally safeguarding your privacy.

Crafting Digital Fortification

Securing your digital devices involves a meticulous blend of encryption, counter-forensic techniques, and strategic evasion of government surveillance. By implementing encryption essentials, adopting counter-forensics practices, and avoiding government surveillance, you are crafting a digital fortress that aligns with your commitment to complete invisibility. Regular audits, staying informed about emerging threats, and adapting to evolving privacy landscapes are imperative for maintaining a resilient defense in the dynamic digital environment.

Chapter 6: Crossing Borders and Blending In

The siren song of freedom beckons beyond the familiar shores. Escape, however, demands not just vanishing, but rebirth. This chapter guides you through the perilous art of crossing borders and blending in, transforming you from a ghost on the run to a chameleon within your chosen haven.

Choosing Your Escape Destination:

Disappearance thrives on misdirection. Choosing your new home isn't just about geography; it's about crafting a narrative that seamlessly integrates you into your surroundings. Consider these factors:

- Visas and Entry Requirements: Prioritize nations offering easy visa access or relaxed immigration policies for your chosen identity. Research work permits, residency options, and potential pitfalls before setting your sights.

- Cultural Similarities: Minimize the cultural chasm you must bridge. Consider societies aligned with your background, language skills, and preferred lifestyle. The easier you blend, the less you'll stand out.

- Cost of Living: Ensure your financial resources can sustain your new life. Factor in the cost of essentials, hidden expenses, and any potential income streams you have established. Remember, invisibility doesn't thrive on empty pockets.

- Privacy and Security: Prioritize countries with strong privacy laws and limited government surveillance. Consider factors like digital freedom, data protection regulations, and the general social climate towards anonymity.

Canada: The Great White North Awaits:

For those seeking pristine landscapes and open arms, Canada beckons. Its Express Entry program offers a swift path to permanent residency for skilled professionals, while working holiday visas provide temporary havens for adventurous spirits. The multicultural tapestry of its cities welcomes diverse backgrounds, and the vast, sparsely populated regions offer ample room for quiet solitude. However, be prepared for harsh winters and higher living costs in major urban centers.

Thailand: Island Hopping in Southeast Asia:

Sun-kissed beaches, laid-back vibes, and a relatively inexpensive cost of living make Thailand a haven for budget-conscious escapees. Visa exemptions for several nationalities and readily available long-term visas facilitate extended stays. The thriving expat community provides support networks and potential employment opportunities. However, navigating language barriers and adapting to the cultural nuances can require patience and cultural sensitivity.

China: Going Incognito in the Dragon's Den:

For the truly intrepid, China presents a unique challenge and potential reward. Its booming economy offers lucrative opportunities for skilled professionals, and its diverse landscape caters to varying preferences. However, strict surveillance systems and a complex bureaucratic apparatus demand extreme caution and meticulous planning. Mastering Mandarin and understanding local customs are crucial for blending in seamlessly. Remember, navigating this dragon's den requires both courage and cunning.

Vietnam

Vietnam can be a much better option for hiding and achieving incognito status compared to China. Here's why:

Surveillance and Freedom:

- China: Boasts a sophisticated and pervasive surveillance system with facial recognition, social media monitoring, and a robust digital infrastructure. For someone seeking true invisibility, this omnipresent gaze can be highly restrictive and make blending in significantly harder.

- Vietnam: While not surveillance-free, the system pales in comparison to China's. Public cameras are less prevalent, social media monitoring is less stringent, and internet censorship, while present, is mainly focused on political content. This creates a more forgiving environment for maintaining anonymity.

Cost of Living and Ease of Integration:

- China: While living costs vary vastly within China, major cities can be quite expensive, especially with the added burden of navigating cultural complexities and potentially needing Mandarin fluency.

- Vietnam: The cost of living in Vietnam is significantly lower, making it more budget-friendly for extended stays or establishing a new life. Additionally, the Vietnamese culture is more open to foreigners, and English is becoming increasingly common in tourist areas and larger cities. This accessibility eases integration and reduces the dependence on mastering a new language.

Visa Options and Bureaucracy:

- China: Obtaining long-term visas in China can be a complex and often frustrating process, requiring substantial documentation, financial proof, and potential language requirements.

- Vietnam: Visa options in Vietnam are generally more straightforward, with tourist visas offering longer stays than China, and easier pathways to obtaining work permits or residency for those with the right skills or investments.

Overall:

While both countries offer their advantages, Vietnam provides a more fertile ground for achieving true incognito status and building a new life under the radar. The relative lack of invasive surveillance, lower cost of living, welcoming cultural climate, and easier visa options make it a superior choice for those seeking freedom and anonymity.

In addition to the points above, consider these further benefits of Vietnam:

- Geographic diversity: From bustling cities to stunning beaches and mountain ranges, Vietnam caters to a variety of desired lifestyles.

- Growing expat community: A thriving expat community in Vietnam offers support networks, potential employment opportunities, and valuable insights into navigating the local culture.

- Entrepreneurial environment: Vietnam's burgeoning economy welcomes foreign investment and entrepreneurial ventures, creating potential sources of income for those seeking to build new lives.

Remember, thorough research and careful planning are still crucial regardless of your chosen destination. Consult professionals, gather reliable information, and assess your specific needs and resources before making your final decision.

Useful Resources:

- VisaGuide.World: https://visaguide.world/

- NomadList: https://nomadlist.com/faq

- ExpatForum: https://www.expatforum.com/

- International Living: https://internationalliving.com/

Remember: Research, research, research! This section provides a high-level overview, but each country demands in-depth investigation into specific visa requirements, cultural norms, economic realities, and potential security risks. Seek professional guidance from immigration specialists and consult reliable sources to ensure your chosen haven truly aligns with your needs and resources.

The journey beyond the border is just the beginning. The next chapter, 7. Mastering the Art of Deception, equips you with the tools to craft a convincing cover story and navigate the social landscape of your new life. Remember, invisibility is just the first step; true mastery lies in becoming one with your surroundings

PART 3: LIVING UNDER THE RADAR

CHAPTER 7: MASTERING THE ART OF DECEPTION

In the pursuit of complete invisibility, mastering the art of deception becomes a crucial skill. This chapter delves into the intricacies of creating a new identity, maintaining your cover story, and avoiding social faux pas to ensure a seamless integration into the chosen environment.

Creating a New Identity

Identity Elements

Establishing a new identity involves careful consideration of key elements:

1. **Name:**

- Choose a name that is common in the host country, blending in with local naming conventions.

- Avoid names that may draw unnecessary attention or scrutiny.

2. **Background Story:**

- Develop a plausible background story that aligns with the cultural and social norms of the host country.

- Consider creating a backstory that involves a job, education, and personal experiences that are common in the local context.

3. **Documentation:**

- Acquire or create legal documentation supporting your new identity, such as identification cards, driver's licenses, or other relevant documents.

- Ensure the documents are consistent with your chosen identity to avoid suspicion.

Appearance Alteration

Modify your appearance to enhance your new identity:

1. **Clothing Style:**

   - Embrace the local fashion to blend in seamlessly.

   - Avoid clothing choices that might be associated with tourists or foreigners.

2. **Hairstyle and Grooming:**

   - Adopt a hairstyle and grooming routine common in the local culture.

   - Regularly update your appearance to maintain a contemporary and inconspicuous look.

3. **Language Accent:**

- Work on acquiring the local accent to enhance linguistic camouflage.

- Practice speaking in a manner consistent with the regional dialect and intonation.

Maintaining Your Cover Story

Consistency is Key

Ensure consistency across all aspects of your cover story:

1. **Job and Education History:**

   - Memorize the details of your fictional job and education history to maintain consistency in conversations.

   - Be prepared to provide additional information if questioned.

2. **Social Connections:**

- Establish and maintain consistent social connections to validate your cover story.

- Integrate seamlessly into local communities to build a network that supports your narrative.

3. **Online Presence:**

   - Create a plausible online presence that aligns with your cover story.

   - Manage social media accounts and profiles in a manner consistent with your new identity.

Handling Inquiries

Be prepared to address inquiries without arousing suspicion:

1. **Confidence in Responses:**

   - Respond confidently to questions about your background, job, or personal history.

- Practice your responses to appear natural and unrehearsed.

2. **Knowledge of Local Culture:**

- Acquire knowledge about local customs, traditions, and current events to contribute to conversations authentically.

- Engage in cultural activities to enhance your understanding of the host community.

3. **Selective Information Sharing:**

- Share information selectively and avoid divulging unnecessary details.

- Be cautious about discussing controversial topics or sensitive issues.

Avoiding Social Faux Pas

Cultural Sensitivity

Navigate social interactions with cultural sensitivity:

1. **Observation and Adaptation:**

   - Observe social norms and adapt your behavior accordingly to avoid standing out.

   - Respect local customs and traditions to integrate seamlessly.

2. **Etiquette Awareness:**

   - Familiarize yourself with local etiquette, including greetings, gestures, and interpersonal boundaries.

   - Avoid actions that may be perceived as disrespectful or offensive.

3. **Understanding Social Hierarchy:**

   - Grasp the nuances of social hierarchy and maintain a level of deference appropriate for your perceived status.

- Avoid behaviors that may be interpreted as challenging societal norms.

Building Trust

Establish trust within your social circles:

1. **Reliability:**

   - Demonstrate reliability in your commitments and actions to build trust.

   - Uphold promises and agreements to reinforce your credibility.

2. **Active Listening:**

   - Practice active listening to understand the nuances of conversations and respond appropriately.

   - Avoid interrupting others and show genuine interest in their perspectives.

3. **Participation in Community Activities:**

    - Participate in community activities and events to showcase your commitment to integration.

    - Contribute positively to communal efforts to gain acceptance.

Mastering Deception Artfully

Mastering the art of deception requires finesse, adaptability, and an acute awareness of the cultural and social dynamics of the host country. By creating a new identity with meticulous attention to detail, maintaining a consistent cover story, and navigating social interactions with cultural sensitivity, you can artfully blend into your chosen environment. Remember, ethical considerations should always guide your actions, and the ultimate goal is to integrate responsibly and respectfully into the community.

CHAPTER 8: SECURING YOUR FINANCES

Invisibility might be your shield, but financial stability is your sword. This chapter equips you with the knowledge and tools to secure your income and navigate the financial landscape without jeopardizing your newfound freedom. Remember, independence thrives on resourcefulness, not empty pockets.

Laundering Money Like a Pro (Legally, of Course):

Let's dispel the myth: true money laundering involves illegal activities and should be avoided at all costs. However, "laundering" your income in the legal sense refers to optimizing your finances for maximum privacy and minimizing unwanted scrutiny. Here are some ethical strategies:

- Embrace Transparency: Document your income through legitimate channels like freelance contracts, consulting fees, or online sales platforms. Maintain detailed records and pay your taxes diligently. This creates a clean paper trail, shielding you from suspicion.

- Ditch the Cash: While tempting, carrying large amounts of cash attracts unwanted attention and limits your options. Utilize bank accounts with international access and consider cryptocurrency wallets for secure, portable wealth (remember, research and understand the risks involved).

- Diversify Your Income Streams: Relying on a single source of income leaves you vulnerable. Explore alternative streams like passive income through investments, royalties, or online businesses. Think of it as spreading your eggs across multiple nests.

- Embrace Barter and Sharing Economies: Sharing resources and skills can significantly reduce your reliance on traditional currency. Consider bartering services, participating in co-housing communities, or utilizing platforms like time

banks. Remember, sometimes the best things in life are free, or at least free-ish.

Disappearing doesn't have to equal deprivation. Here are some tips for minimizing your financial footprint while maintaining a comfortable lifestyle:

- Embrace Minimalism: Downsize your possessions and learn to live with less. This reduces physical clutter and minimizes storage costs, allowing you to move with greater ease and flexibility.

- Go DIY: Master basic skills like cooking, repairing clothes, or growing your own food. This reduces dependence on consumer goods and empowers you to become self-sufficient.

- Explore Alternative Housing: Consider unconventional living options like tiny houses, caravans, or eco-friendly self-builds. These often offer lower costs and greater freedom from traditional mortgages and rent burdens.

- Seek Community: Collaborate with like-minded individuals to share resources, skills, and living spaces. Community co-ops, intentional living communities, and off-grid collectives can offer support and reduce individual expenses.

Alternative Income Streams:

Traditional employment can leave a digital trail and limit your location flexibility. Consider these alternative income sources for a life off the beaten financial path:

- Freelancing and Remote Work: Offer your skills and expertise online in fields like writing, programming, design, or consulting. Platforms like Upwork, Fiverr, and Nomad

List open doors to global clients and location independence.

- Online Businesses: Build an online presence through e-commerce stores, educational courses, or digital products. The internet offers a vast, borderless marketplace where your creativity can generate sustainable income.

- Passive Income Investments: Explore low-risk investments like index funds, rental properties, or royalty-generating creative works. The goal is to build streams of income that require minimal active effort.

- Skill Sharing and Workshops: Teach your unique skills and knowledge through online and offline workshops, courses, or mentoring programs. Turn your expertise into a valuable commodity.

Remember: Financial security is a journey, not a destination. Adapt your strategies to your changing circumstances and needs. Continuous learning, resourcefulness, and a willingness to break free from conventional income models are your keys to navigating the off-grid financial landscape.

Remember, true disappearance thrives not just on vanishing, but on becoming someone, or many someones, entirely new.

CHAPTER 9: EVERYDAY DISAPPEARANCE

In the pursuit of an invisible existence, mastering the art of everyday disappearance is essential. This chapter provides comprehensive guidance on travel tips, staying safe in your new life, and maintaining mental health throughout the process.

Travel Tips for the Invisible

Low-Profile Travel Arrangements

1. **Avoid High-Profile Destinations:**

   - Choose travel destinations that are not heavily frequented by tourists or attract attention.

   - Opt for places where blending in is easier, and your presence won't be noteworthy.

2. **Use Public Transportation:**

   - Rely on public transportation to move around inconspicuously.

- Avoid conspicuous modes of travel that might draw attention.

3. **Stay in Local Accommodations:**

   - Opt for local guesthouses or non-chain hotels to minimize visibility.

   - Choose accommodation away from popular tourist areas.

Discreet Documentation

1. **Minimize Paper Trail:**

   - Carry only essential documentation to minimize the paper trail.

   - Use digital copies stored securely whenever possible.

2. **Identity-Blending:**

- Ensure your appearance aligns with the local population to avoid standing out.

- Be cautious when presenting identification, especially in places with strict regulations.

3. **Local SIM Cards:**

- Use local SIM cards for communication to avoid international attention.

- Be aware of local regulations regarding SIM card registration.

Staying Safe and Sound in Your New Life

Security Measures

1. **Securing Living Spaces:**

- Choose accommodations with secure entry and privacy features.

- Install basic security measures, such as door and window locks.

2. **Routine Changes:**

   - Vary your routines to avoid predictability.

   - Be cautious about establishing recognizable patterns in your daily activities.

3. **Emergency Plans:**

   - Develop emergency exit plans for various scenarios.

   - Know the location of local embassies or consulates for assistance.

Networking with Caution

1. **Selectively Building Connections:**

   - Be selective in forming social connections, focusing on individuals you can trust.

- Avoid divulging unnecessary personal details to new acquaintances.

2. **Maintaining a Low Profile:**

- Cultivate a low-profile online presence to minimize exposure.

3. **Assessing Trustworthiness:**

- Assess the trustworthiness of individuals before sharing sensitive information.

- Trust is earned over time; exercise caution in forming close bonds.

Mental Health and the Disappeared

Coping with Isolation

1. **Engaging in Hobbies:**

- Develop and nurture personal hobbies to fill leisure time.

- Engaging in activities you enjoy can contribute to a sense of fulfillment.

2. **Mindful Practices:**

   - Incorporate mindfulness practices into your routine to manage stress.

   - Meditation and relaxation techniques can aid in maintaining mental well-being.

3. **Establishing Virtual Connections:**

   - Maintain virtual connections with trusted friends or family members.

   - Regular communication can provide emotional support and combat feelings of isolation.

Seeking Professional Support

1. **Accessing Local Services:**

- Familiarize yourself with local mental health services and resources.

- Know where to seek professional help if needed.

2. **Online Counseling:**

- Explore online counseling services for remote mental health support.

- Maintain a connection with mental health professionals who understand your unique circumstances.

3. **Cultivating Resilience:**

- Develop resilience through self-awareness and adaptive coping strategies.

- Embrace challenges as opportunities for personal growth.

Mastering Everyday Disappearance

Mastering the art of everyday disappearance requires a delicate balance between blending into the background and ensuring personal well-being. By following travel tips that emphasize low-profile arrangements, staying safe through security measures, and prioritizing mental health, you can navigate the challenges of an invisible existence with resilience and mindfulness. Remember, maintaining a healthy state of mind is paramount in the pursuit of a discreet and fulfilling life.

CONCLUSION

You've shed the layers, erased the footprints, and embraced the shadows. This journey through invisibility has equipped you with the knowledge and tools to vanish from sight, both physically and digitally. But as you stand teetering on the precipice of your new life, a final question echoes: can such disappearance be eternal?

Is Anonymity Forever?:

The harsh reality is, complete and permanent anonymity remains a tantalizing mirage in the desert of reality. Technology evolves, governments persist, and memories linger. Your past, however skillfully buried, could resurface under the relentless glare of determined pursuit or unforeseen circumstances. However, true invisibility isn't about absolute obscurity; it's about managing risk, mitigating exposure, and adapting to the ever-shifting sands of the surveillance landscape.

The Cost of Disappearance:

The price of invisibility is not paid solely in digital coins or discarded identities. It carries a subtle weight on your soul, a constant awareness of the chasm between your past and present. Relationships may fade, connections may sever, and a familiar pang of nostalgia for simpler times might rise from the ashes of your former life. Remember, disappearance is not just a tactical maneuver; it's an emotional tightrope walk, demanding balance and resilience.

The Final Fade:

This book is not an endpoint, but a compass, guiding you through the initial steps of crafting your invisibility. The final fade, however, is yours to orchestrate. Whether you disappear into the bustling anonymity of a megacity, forge a new life under the sun-drenched skies of a foreign land, or retreat to the quiet solitude of the uncharted wilds, remember this: invisibility is not a destination, but a continuous performance. Embrace the fluidity, remain vigilant, and never underestimate the power of reinvention.

As you slip into the shadows, cast one last glance at the light you leave behind. It's not a rejection, but a redirection. You are not lost; you are reborn. This is not the end; it's the beginning of your invisible masterpiece.

Go forth, vanish, and rewrite your narrative. The canvas of invisibility awaits.

Farewell. May your shadows be long and your freedom boundless.

Bonus Chapter

In the quest for invisibility, a myriad of ethical considerations surfaces, prompting contemplation on the boundaries of personal privacy, societal responsibility, and the potential consequences of going off the grid. This bonus chapter delves into the ethical implications of adopting a lifestyle that embraces invisibility, exploring the nuances of when it may go too far.

The Concept of Ethical Invisibility

Understanding Personal Privacy

The concept of personal privacy has evolved in the digital age, where individuals willingly share vast amounts of personal information online. Ethical invisibility begins with the right to control one's personal information, and proponents argue that the pursuit of privacy is a fundamental human right. Choosing to be invisible can be seen as an assertion of this right, especially in the face of pervasive surveillance and data collection.

Societal Implications

However, ethical considerations extend beyond individual rights to encompass the impact of disappearing on a societal level. Communities thrive on shared responsibilities, and when individuals choose complete invisibility, questions arise about their contributions to the collective well-being. Can one ethically detach from societal responsibilities while enjoying the benefits of communal structures?

The Thin Line: When Does It Go Too Far?

Legal Boundaries

One crucial aspect of ethical invisibility involves respecting legal boundaries. Going off the grid should not involve engaging in illegal activities, such as identity theft, fraud, or money laundering. Maintaining ethical invisibility necessitates adherence to the laws of the host country, and crossing legal lines can lead to severe consequences.

Responsibility to Others

Consideration must be given to the impact of disappearing on family and friends. When does the pursuit of personal privacy infringe upon the emotional well-being of those left behind? Ethical boundaries dictate a responsibility to communicate intentions, especially when the choice to disappear affects the lives of others.

Environmental Impact

The environmental impact of an invisible lifestyle also falls within the realm of ethical considerations. Sustainability practices often require accountability, and disappearing can pose challenges to responsible environmental stewardship. Balancing the desire for invisibility with eco-friendly practices becomes a delicate ethical dance.

Ethical Dilemmas in Invisibility Practices

112

The Fine Line Between Privacy and Secrecy

One ethical dilemma arises in distinguishing between a desire for privacy and a propensity for secrecy. While individuals have the right to a private life, a line is crossed when secrecy involves activities that pose harm to oneself or others. Deciphering the boundary between personal privacy and potential harm is a central ethical challenge.

Balancing Autonomy and Accountability

Ethical invisibility demands a nuanced understanding of autonomy and accountability. While individuals have the autonomy to shape their lives as they see fit, ethical considerations require a balance that acknowledges societal accountability. Striking this balance involves mindful decisions that respect personal autonomy without neglecting responsibilities to others.

The Tension Between Freedom and Community

The pursuit of complete invisibility can be viewed as an assertion of freedom, yet it raises questions about the responsibilities individuals have to their communities. Ethical dilemmas emerge when personal freedom clashes with the collective needs of society. How much freedom is too much, and when does personal choice become a detriment to community well-being?

Mitigating Ethical Concerns: A Responsible Approach to Invisibility

Transparent Communication

One way to address ethical concerns is through transparent communication. Individuals considering the path of invisibility should communicate openly with loved ones about their intentions. This transparency enables a shared understanding and minimizes potential emotional fallout.

Legal Compliance

Maintaining ethical invisibility necessitates strict adherence to legal boundaries. Individuals must navigate their disappearing acts within the confines of the law, ensuring that their pursuit of privacy does not involve any illegal activities or infringe upon the rights of others.

Environmental Responsibility

Environmental impact can be mitigated through conscientious choices. Embracing sustainable practices, minimizing waste, and actively contributing to eco-friendly initiatives can help offset the potential environmental footprint of an invisible lifestyle.

Balancing Autonomy and Responsibility

Striking a balance between personal autonomy and responsibility to others requires mindfulness and self-reflection. Ethical invisibility should not be pursued at the expense of interpersonal relationships and societal contributions. Individuals must weigh the benefits of personal privacy against the responsibilities they owe to their communities.

Conclusion: Navigating the Ethical Landscape of Invisibility

In the complex terrain of ethical invisibility, individuals must navigate a landscape fraught with dilemmas and responsibilities. Recognizing the fine line between personal privacy and societal accountability is crucial for those considering disappearing from the conventional grid. Striking a balance between autonomy and responsibility, transparency in communication, legal compliance, and environmental responsibility can pave the way for an ethical approach to invisibility. Ultimately, the pursuit of personal privacy should be guided by a conscientious understanding of the broader implications, acknowledging that the ethical boundaries of invisibility are as nuanced as the individuals who embark on this unique journey.

www.ingramcontent.com/pod-product-compliance
Lightning Source LLC
Chambersburg PA
CBHW072316290526
45794CB00002B/686